CW01431804

Original title:

Umber Leaves Over the Unicorn Husk

Author: Liisi Lendorav

ISBN HARDBACK: 978-1-80559-485-7

ISBN PAPERBACK: 978-1-80559-984-5

Autumn's Whispering Elegance

Leaves of amber drift and sway,
A soft gust whispers them away.
Branches bare, in twilight glow,
Nature's beauty starts to slow.

Golden hues on gentle ground,
In this silence, peace is found.
A crispness lingers in the air,
Autumn's grace is everywhere.

Enchanted Echoes of the Forest

Whispers dance among the trees,
Carried softly by the breeze.
A melody of rustling leaves,
Nature's song that never leaves.

Mossy banks hold secrets deep,
Where shadows of the ancients creep.
Every sound a tale unfolds,
In twilight's arm, the magic holds.

The Last Dance of Golden Foliage

Foliage spins in a final dance,
Fleeting moments, a last chance.
Crimson and gold, a fading show,
As winter's breath begins to blow.

Beneath the trees, the whispers sigh,
A farewell under the sunset's eye.
Nature's cycle, a sacred trance,
In the twilight, they take their chance.

Reflections in the Glade's Embrace

Mirrored stillness in the pond,
Where dreams and reality respond.
Fragrant blooms and mossy beds,
The whispers of the past it treads.

Beneath the boughs, a safe retreat,
Echoes of life in each heartbeat.
The glade holds stories untold,
In its embrace, warmth unfolds.

Legends Carried by the Autumn Breeze

Whispers glide through rustling leaves,
Tales of old that nature weaves.
Each golden hue, a story spread,
Of heroes past, long gone but led.

Beneath the trees, where shadows play,
Legends breathe in the cool decay.
With every gust, a voice resounds,
Echoes of life, in nature found.

The crows caw loud, the winds reply,
Fables dance beneath the sky.
A tapestry of time unfolds,
In autumn's grasp, the past retold.

Through harvest fields, the spirits roam,
In every rustle, memory's home.
Corn stalks bow to the stories shared,
In twilight's glow, the world has dared.

So let the breeze recite the lore,
Of times and places, evermore.
For every breeze that sweeps the land,
Holds a legend, a timeless strand.

When Nature's Melodies Meet the Muse

In a garden where secrets bloom,
Nature sings, dispelling gloom.
Birds perform on branches high,
Each note a spark, like stars in sky.

The river hums a gentle tune,
Beneath the watchful, glowing moon.
Leaves sway softly, a graceful dance,
Inviting hearts to take a chance.

The breeze carries a soft refrain,
Reminding souls of joy and pain.
Blossoms whisper to the winds,
In every petal, a tale begins.

Colors mingle, a painter's dream,
Where every shadow casts a gleam.
Nature's hand, an artist bold,
Weaves harmony, both new and old.

So listen close, let spirits flow,
In nature's song, let passions grow.
For when the muse and earth collide,
A symphony of life abides.

Whispers of Autumn Embers

Leaves cascade in hues of gold,
A tapestry of stories told.
Gentle winds begin to sigh,
As seasons fade and dreams drift by.

Fires crackle in a distant glow,
Soft echoes of warmth below.
With every flicker, whispers rise,
Painting memories in the skies.

Cider brews in copper pots,
The world in amber, time forgot.
Footsteps crunch on fallen ground,
In autumn's arms, solace found.

Misty mornings softly gleam,
Nature sighs, a waking dream.
In twilight's hush, the shadows play,
As embers dance and fade away.

The Enchanted Hearth's Palette

In the hearth, the colors glow,
Crimson reds and golden flow.
A painter's dream in warmth unfolds,
The stories of the heart retold.

Brush strokes made of fire's kiss,
Each flicker a moment's bliss.
Softly swaying, shadows crawl,
As warmth envelops one and all.

Through crackling flames, the spirits sing,
Weaving tales on restless wing.
With every spark, a vision clear,
Of love and laughter drawing near.

The hearth a canvas, life's embrace,
Where memories dance, and fears erase.
A tapestry of heart and soul,
In the enchanted glow, we're whole.

Secrets of the Woodland Canopy

In the forest, shadows weave,
Whispers linger, tales believe.
Branches stretch with stories old,
A world of wonder to behold.

Sunlight filters, soft and bright,
Bathing leaves in golden light.
Every rustle, every sigh,
Holds the secrets of the sky.

Beneath the boughs, the wild things play,
Nature's children, night and day.
In this realm, a magic thrives,
Where every heartbeat softly dives.

Mossy carpets cradle feet,
In shadows deep, the lost hearts meet.
The canopy, a loving shroud,
Keeps our dreams within its crowd.

A Dance of Amber and Mystique

Golden hues beneath the trees,
Dancing lightly with the breeze.
Twilight whispers secrets low,
As the stars begin to glow.

Amber worlds in shadow's clasp,
Nature's breath in twilight's gasp.
Each flicker, each glowing spark,
Illuminates the lurking dark.

A waltz of fireflies takes flight,
In the embrace of the night.
Mystique lingers, soft and sweet,
With each heartbeat, life's heartbeat.

Together, nature sings her hymn,
In amber beams, the light feels dim.
A dance of spirits in the quiet,
Whispering secrets, no one tries it.

An Ode to the Wondrous Unknown

In a world where shadows dance,
Secrets whisper, fate's advance.
Each step taken, paths unfold,
Mysteries new, stories told.

Stars above in twilight gleam,
Guiding those who dream a dream.
The heart yearns to seek and find,
What lies beyond, fresh and unkind.

Through the fog, the echoes call,
Inviting souls to brave the thrall.
With every breath, the night so deep,
Awakens wonders lost in sleep.

Every corner hides a tale,
In the night, the shadows sail.
Embrace the fear, the thrill unknown,
In the dark, we're never alone.

An ode sung to paths unseen,
Where the wild and soft convene.
Together we shall seek, we'll roam,
In the unknown, we find our home.

Tales Strung on the Forest's Breath

Whispers thread through trees so tall,
Ancient tales in twilight call.
Leaves a'sway with secrets bare,
Nature speaks, the soul laid bare.

Mossy carpets, rich and deep,
Where the woodland creatures leap.
Every rustle, every sigh,
Holds a memory passing by.

Sunlight filters, shadows play,
Painting pathways where we stray.
In the heart of emerald halls,
Adventure waits as silence falls.

Footfalls soft on forest floor,
Open hearts will find the door.
Each encounter, vivid, bright,
Stories sung in nature's light.

Echoed laughter, friendship's thread,
Binding lives where we are led.
With the forest, hand in hand,
Tales of wonder, boldly stand.

Colors of Enchantment in Gilded Shadows

In twilight's hug, the colors blend,
Magenta skies, horizons bend.
Leaves like jewels catch the gaze,
Enchanted hue in evening's haze.

Crimson whispers, golden flare,
Brush of beauty everywhere.
In the dusk, where dreams ignite,
Shadows dance with pure delight.

Violet shades and sapphire gleam,
Filling hearts with vibrant dreams.
In each corner, magic brews,
Nature's palette, fresh and new.

Every moment, fleeting glance,
Urgent heartbeats, tangled chance.
In gilded realms, the spirits soar,
Embracing colors, we explore.

Painting life with every breath,
Crafting joy amidst the depth.
In this canvas, vast and wide,
Live the colors, let them guide.

The Paradigm of Autumn's Gift

Crisp the air, the leaves descend,
Nature's cycle, summer's end.
Burnished golds and auburn hues,
Paint the ground, a feast of views.

Harvest moons and longer nights,
Gathering warmth in cozy sights.
Every whisper of the breeze,
Carries tales of ancient trees.

Pumpkin patches, cider sweet,
Echoes of a rhythmic beat.
In the fields, life takes a pause,
Nature's bounty, just because.

With each leaf that swirls to ground,
New beginnings can be found.
The promise held in twilight's glow,
Is a path where seasons flow.

Embrace the chill, the fading sun,
In autumn's heart, we all are one.
In every chill, the warmth we find,
The paradigm of heart and mind.

When Magic Dances in the Autumn Breeze

Golden leaves twirl down,
Soft whispers in the air.
The world in colors found,
Nature's gentle flair.

Crisp is the evening light,
As shadows start to play.
Enchantments take their flight,
In twilight's warm embrace.

The trees sway with delight,
With secrets to declare.
Stars emerge in full sight,
Their glimmers everywhere.

A hush falls on the night,
As crickets serenade.
The moon, a silver kite,
In skies of deep cascade.

Magic weaves through the scene,
In every rustling sound.
With hearts alive and keen,
In autumn's spell, we're bound.

Chronicles of Rustling Fables and Whispers

Beneath the ancient oaks,
Where stories softly blend,
The wind, a voice that hoax,
With tales that never end.

Leaves dance with fervent grace,
Each rustle holds a clue.
In nature's warm embrace,
Old fables come anew.

Creatures gather around,
To listen, hearts aglow.
In whispers, magic found,
From roots to branches grow.

Moonlight writes the lore,
On paths where shadows creep.
Each secret holds the core,
Of dreams that dance in sleep.

Chronicles alive,
In every fleeting sound.
With wonder, we thrive,
In whispers all around.

The Unicorn's Prism in the Forest's Heart

Deep in the forest's core,
Where sunlight barely gleams,
Lives a creature of lore,
In a world of dreams.

Its mane, a brilliant hue,
Like rainbows in the mist.
With eyes that shine so true,
In starlight, it exists.

Through reeds and verdant trails,
The whispers call it near.
With grace, the unicorn sails,
In shadows, crystal clear.

Every step, a delight,
Each breath, a gentle sigh.
It dances through the night,
An echo in the sky.

The forest holds its breath,
As magic takes its part.
Life blooms beyond the death,
In the unicorn's heart.

Crimson Hues and Twilit Reveries

Crimson streaks light the path,
As daylight starts to fade.
Whispers of the aftermath,
In twilight's soft parade.

Stars peek from their curtains,
As dusk begins to sing.
The sky, a hue of burdens,
Where dreams take flight on wing.

In gardens, shadows play,
With colors rich and bold.
Memories drift away,
In stories yet untold.

Each breath is filled with peace,
As night begins to fall.
In dreams, we find release,
Heed the night's gentle call.

In crimson's soft embrace,
And reveries, we find,
The magic of this space,
Unfolds in heart and mind.

Beyond the Gates of Autumn's Wonderland

Leaves fall gently, gold and red,
Whispers of wind, softly said.
Crisp air dances, cold and bright,
Days grow shorter, fading light.

Misty mornings, dawn's embrace,
Nature's magic, cherished space.
Pumpkin patches, laughter loud,
Joyful hearts, we stand so proud.

Harvest moon, a watchful eye,
Beneath its glow, we dream and sigh.
Fields of plenty, stories told,
In this season, hearts turned gold.

Fireplace crackles, warmth inside,
Memories gather, hearts abide.
Through the gates, we wander far,
Guided by the evening star.

Together sharing, moments sweet,
In autumn's wonder, love must meet.
Beyond the gates, our spirits soar,
In this season, we seek more.

Serenity Wrapped in Nature's Loom

Beneath the trees, a soft caress,
Nature's heart, a gentle dress.
Birds in chorus, sing their song,
In this silence, we belong.

Rivers whisper secrets low,
Flowing softly, never slow.
Mountains stand with tranquil grace,
Guardians of this sacred place.

Meadows bloom with colors bright,
Kissed by sun, a pure delight.
Time stands still, breaths entwine,
In this realm, our souls align.

Clouds drift lazily on high,
Painting dreams across the sky.
Nature cradles, tender hold,
In every moment, life unfolds.

Harmony in every leaf,
A refuge found, beyond belief.
Wrapped in love, the world anew,
In nature's embrace, just us two.

Opalescent Echoes of Nature's Breath

Morning dew on cobwebs glint,
Nature's art, a fleeting hint.
Softly rustling leaves align,
Swaying gently, all divine.

Mirrored lakes reflect the sky,
Where dreams linger, never shy.
Whispers of the evening breeze,
Carrying secrets through the trees.

In twilight's glow, shadows play,
Painting night from end of day.
Stars emerge, a silent choir,
Igniting hearts with soft desire.

Crickets sing their lullabies,
Underneath the starlit skies.
In these echoes, we feel free,
Nature's breath, a memory.

We wander through this sacred space,
In opalescent dreams we trace.
Each moment rich, each heartbeat true,
In nature's song, forever new.

Stories Spun in the Dusk's Glare

Sunset whispers tales untold,
In hues of fiery orange gold.
Dusk arrives, a gentle sigh,
Veiling the world, bidding goodbye.

Shadows stretch in quiet grace,
While stars awaken in their place.
The moon ascends, a silver seam,
Weaving through our nightly dream.

Crickets chirp their evening song,
In the dusk, where we belong.
Fires crackle, stories shared,
In the warmth, we know we cared.

Beneath the canopy of dark,
Life ignites, a vibrant spark.
With each heartbeat, tales abound,
In the dusk's embrace, we're found.

Time drifts softly, moments flow,
In the night's embrace, we grow.
Stories spun in softest glare,
In the dusk's light, hearts lay bare.

Where Echoes of Myth and Nature Converge

In the valley where shadows play,
Ancient tales weave night and day,
Whispers of gods in the brook's flow,
Roots of history beneath the glow.

Mountains guard secrets of old,
Legends alive in the silence bold,
Rivers hum songs of forgotten grace,
Nature's arms embrace this space.

Moonlight dances on leaves so green,
Spirit of forest, serene, unseen,
Echoes ring through the emerald wood,
Bound by the threads of all that stood.

Where rocks recount stories untold,
And winds carry dreams, both young and old,
Moments blend like colors in the air,
A harmony forged beyond compare.

Here in the stillness, time stands still,
In every corner, a forgotten thrill,
Where echoes of myth and nature sing,
Life entwined in the joy they bring.

Enigma of Leaves in the Whispering Wind

Leaves murmur softly in twilight's breath,
Carried by breezes, life finds its heft,
Secrets flutter in each verdant hue,
Nature's whispers, mysterious and true.

Dancing with shadows, they twist and twine,
Under the stars where the world aligns,
Enigmas hidden in rustling sound,
Stories awakened, longing unbound.

With each gust, memories drift and sway,
As soft as the dusk that fades away,
The pulse of the earth in every line,
Leaves weave their tale, both yours and mine.

Fleeting moments, like petals they fall,
The wind's caress holds the answers to all,
In the hush of the dusk, secrets reside,
Leaves not alone, but joined in the tide.

Enigma unfolds in the sounds we heed,
Nature's language, the heart's gentle plead,
In harmony found where whispers may glide,
The world spins slowly, in dreams we confide.

The Goddess of Fall: Keeper of the Thicket

In the amber glow of the autumn eve,
A goddess dances with leaves that weave,
Crimson and gold, a fiery blend,
In the thicket's embrace, blessings descend.

She gathers whispers from branches high,
With a joy that glistens in the darkening sky,
Her laughter rings in the chilly breeze,
Caressing the earth with a gentle tease.

Each leaf a promise, each gust a sign,
Nature's bounty, forever divine,
A guardian of beauty as seasons change,
In her thicket, the wild feels strange.

With roots entwined in a sacred ground,
The stories of nature in her heart are found,
She nurtures the earth with a tender hand,
Guiding the rhythm of life's great band.

As twilight settles, shadows unfurl,
The goddess weaves magic in every swirl,
Keeper of cycles, unseen and wise,
In her presence, the spirit flies.

Dappled Light in a World Apart

Sunlight filters through branches bright,
Creating patterns of softness and light,
Dappled shadows where dreams may start,
In a quiet realm, set worlds apart.

Golden beams dance on the forest floor,
Inviting the wanderer to explore,
Where the melody of nature swells,
And peace resides in the secret wells.

With each step taken on the mossy ground,
Echoes of laughter in silence abound,
The whispers of trees, a soft serenade,
In this refuge, deep joy is laid.

Moments of stillness, a breath of grace,
Time slows down in this sacred space,
Here in the glimmer, the soul ignites,
Dappled light sends us into flights.

In the tender glow of a world apart,
We find the rhythm that beats in the heart,
Nature surrounds with a gentle embrace,
A haven of beauty, our infinite place.

Glade of the Luminescent Muse

In the glade where shadows play,
Soft whispers guide the night away.
Moonlight dances on the leaves,
As gentle winds hum, the heart believes.

Petals glow in silver hues,
Dreams awaken, kissed by dew.
Echoes weave through the fragrant air,
Carrying secrets, tender and rare.

Stars above begin to gleam,
Crafting tales in a starlit dream.
The muse awakens, inspiration flows,
In this serene world, a magic grows.

Branches sway with a mystic grace,
As time stands still in this sacred space.
A symphony of nature's song,
Calls forth the artist, proud and strong.

With every breath, the heart ignites,
In the glade of soft, enchanted nights.
The luminescent muse, so bright and true,
Wraps the world in a vibrant hue.

When the World Turns Russet

When the world turns russet and gold,
Stories of summer gently unfold.
Leaves burst forth in fiery dance,
Nature wears its autumnal romance.

Cool breezes whisper through the trees,
With a sigh, they hum their melodies.
Crisp air dries the fading sheen,
As earth prepares for the winter's green.

Golden sunlight breaks the silence,
Painting walls with warm defiance.
Fires burn with a crackling cheer,
As cozy moments draw us near.

Time moves slowly, a tender embrace,
As every face finds its rightful place.
In rustling leaves and evening skies,
The heart finds solace, the spirit flies.

When night descends, stars begin to spark,
Illuminating dreams in the dark.
The world, now russet, softly sighs,
As autumn's breath paints lullabies.

Secrets in the Tranquil Embers

In the glow of tranquil embers,
A quiet warmth embraces dreams.
Stories linger in the twilight,
Whispers dance like flowing streams.

Flickering flames tell tales of old,
Of love and loss, of brave and bold.
A gentle hush wraps around softly,
As secrets in the night unfold.

Shadows play on the walls so grand,
Recalling moments, hand in hand.
Every crackle holds a promise,
That time can never truly withstand.

Stars peek through the window's pane,
Reflecting memories, joy, and pain.
In the stillness, hearts connect,
Finding strength to rise again.

With every breath, we seek the light,
In the embers, sparks ignite.
Secrets shared among the flames,
In the tranquility of night.

Whispers of Fall Among the Dappled Light

Whispers of fall among the trees,
Carry tales on the brisk cool breeze.
Leaves cascade in shades so bright,
Nature wraps us in soft twilight.

Dappled light filters through the vast,
Creating memories that forever last.
Time moves gently, a lover's caress,
As every heartbeat finds its rest.

The garden rustles with a serenade,
Melodies in the cool air laid.
In every petal, every hue,
Autumn's canvas comes alive anew.

Beneath the arch of a painted sky,
Dreams take flight and softly lie.
Comfort flows in the golden hour,
And every heartbeat finds its power.

As twilight deepens, shadows play,
Silent prayers at the close of day.
With each breath, the heart takes flight,
In whispers of fall to the soft moonlight.

Where Celestial Beasts Roam in Gloom

In twilight's grasp, shadows weave,
Beasts of legends, none believe.
With silent wings, they glide unseen,
Through ancient woods, where few have been.

Their eyes like stars, in darkness glint,
Whispers linger, soft and faint.
In realms of fog, where spirits sigh,
The echo of a mournful cry.

Beneath the moon's soft, silver light,
They dance in dreams, a wondrous sight.
Through tangled thickets, wild and free,
In haunting beauty, they roam with glee.

In every shadow, a story lies,
Unfolding mysteries in the skies.
Where time stands still, forevermore,
The celestial beasts, they gently soar.

With hearts entwined, as dusk descends,
The night begins where daylight ends.
In realms unknown, where legends bloom,
Beyond the veil, in twilight's gloom.

Shadows at Dusk's Enchanted Edge

As daylight fades, the shadows blend,
Where whispers of the night descend.
On edges where the world grows dim,
Mysteries dance on a twilight whim.

Softly flicker, the lanterns glow,
Through tangled paths where few would go.
In every rustle, secrets call,
To those who heed the evening's thrall.

The moonlit silver paints the trees,
While gentle sighing fills the breeze.
At dusk's embrace, shadows entwine,
In ethereal tales, they softly shine.

Beneath the stars' watchful gaze,
In twilight's magic, hearts ablaze.
A realm where time and dreams unite,
In shadows dancing, pure delight.

So linger not, when light departs,
Embrace the dusk with open hearts.
For in its mysteries, we shall find,
The beauty that the night has lined.

The Rustic Chronicle of Celestial Creatures

In valleys deep, where whispers dwell,
The rustic tales are ours to tell.
Creatures born from starlit dreams,
Woven within the sunlit beams.

Through ancient fields, they roam and play,
In harmony, night meets day.
With nimble grace, they leap and glide,
Beneath the trees, where shadows hide.

In every rustling blade and leaf,
Lies the heart's desire for belief.
The chorus sings, a rustic song,
Of celestial beings, where they belong.

Each creature holds a story bright,
Of moonlit dances, pure delight.
In every encounter, magic flows,
Life's tapestry, woven in prose.

From fields to skies, the tales extend,
A legacy that will not end.
In rustic charm, the creatures dwell,
In tranquil corners, their stories swell.

Hues of Twilight Amongst Mythical Guardians

In twilight's brush, the colors blend,
Mythical guardians, on them depend.
With wings of fire, and hearts of stone,
In hues of dusk, their magic's shown.

They stand as sentinels of night,
Chasing shadows, hunting light.
With gentle care, they guide the way,
Through realms where dreams and spirits play.

Emerald eyes and silver fur,
In every heartbeat, their spirits stir.
Amongst the stars, they weave their fate,
In colors bright, they resonate.

Guardians of dusk, with tales to share,
Of ancient times, and whispered air.
In every flicker, a story spun,
In shades of twilight, they've just begun.

As night unfolds, their magic gleams,
A vibrant dance of silent dreams.
With every breath, the realms ignite,
In hues of twilight, pure delight.

Chamber of Forgotten Creatures

In shadows deep, they hide away,
With stories lost, where spirits play.
Whispers echo in the night,
Of ancient dreams and fading light.

Through cobwebs thick, the memories creep,
Of fleeting glances, secrets kept.
Silent howls in darkness rise,
Underneath the starlit skies.

Each corner holds a breath of lore,
A tale of battles fought before.
In quiet corners, magic stirs,
As time itself begins to purr.

Forgotten beings softly sigh,
In this chamber where shadows lie.
Embers of life once danced so bright,
Now merely whispers in the night.

Yet hope remains, a gentle thread,
To bind the lost to dreams unsaid.
In heartbeats soft, they will return,
In flickering flames, their stories burn.

The Golden Hour's Serenity

The sun hangs low, a golden sphere,
Its gentle warmth draws all near.
Fields aglow in amber light,
Whispering secrets of the night.

Nature breathes in restful sighs,
As day prepares to bid goodbye.
Shadows stretch and dance anew,
In hues of pink and vibrant blue.

A tranquil hush drapes every tree,
As birds in chorus sing with glee.
The world holds its breath, so still,
Beneath the magic of the hill.

Moments catch in twilight's hand,
As dreams unfurl across the land.
In this embrace, hearts intertwine,
In fleeting beauty, love does shine.

As stars awaken, one by one,
The golden hour, now gently done.
In every heart, a glow remains,
A soft reminder of joy's chains.

Reveries Beneath the Boughs of Time

Beneath the boughs, the whispers flow,
Where every leaf holds tales to show.
In twilight's grasp, the echoes sing,
Of bygone days and timeless spring.

Moments linger, softly bright,
In glades where shadows dance with light.
Time stands still, a sacred space,
In nature's arms, we find our grace.

Dreams entwined in nature's weave,
Beneath the boughs, we dare believe.
In every sigh, a story lives,
In every pause, the heart forgives.

Dappled sun on mossy ground,
In this refuge, calm is found.
Whispers of the past align,
In gentle rhythms, hearts combine.

As shadows blend with evening's call,
We lose ourselves, we risk it all.
For in this realm, where time feels right,
We find our dreams in starry night.

Serenade of the Twilight Meadows

In twilight's breath, the meadows sigh,
As colors fade in the evening sky.
Shadows weave through blades of grass,
A gentle dance, as moments pass.

Crickets sing a soft refrain,
While fireflies light the dark like rain.
The world is hushed, a sacred space,
Where time suspends its frantic chase.

Petals close to greet the night,
As stars awaken, pure and bright.
In the coolness, whispers bloom,
Their fragrant tales dispel the gloom.

Every breeze a lover's embrace,
Each rustling leaf, a tender trace.
In harmony, the night unfolds,
With secrets shared and dreams retold.

As moonlight bathes the meadow's grace,
We find our peace in this still place.
A serenade for hearts that roam,
In twilight meadows, we are home.

Whispered Secrets of Mythic Woods

In shadowed glades where whispers dwell,
A tale of old begins to swell.
The moss-clad roots in silence weave,
While ancient spirits dance and grieve.

The moonlight filters through the trees,
In gentle sighs, the night-time breathes.
Each rustling leaf a story told,
Of hero's hearts and treasures bold.

Beneath the stars, the wild dreams play,
Where time stands still and shadows sway.
The echoes call, a siren's hum,
Through tangled paths, the lost may come.

A brook's soft laughter fills the air,
With every turn, a secret's lair.
The petals bloom, a fleeting sight,
In whispered tones of day and night.

As twilight wraps the world in hugs,
The gentle breeze carries soft tugs.
Each secret held, a gem concealed,
In mythic woods where dreams are healed.

The Leafy Ode of Forgotten Realms

Upon the boughs of crumbling lore,
Leaves sing hymns, tales of yore.
In vibrant hues, their voices blend,
A vibrant saga with no end.

Each rustle speaks of past delight,
In hidden realms, beyond our sight.
The branches stretch with stories wide,
Of lands where myths and dreams collide.

With every breeze, memories wake,
In leafy whispers, hearts do ache.
Dance of shadows, flicker, freeze,
Where time flows gently, like the breeze.

A tapestry of colors bright,
In every turn, a new insight.
The roots entwine in silent prayer,
For those who seek the magic there.

In forgotten realms, where echoes play,
The trees hold guard, both night and day.
Their leafy ode, a wondrous plea,
To behold the beauty, wild and free.

In the Wake of Gilded Whispers

As dawn's first light spills gold on dew,
Gilded whispers trace the view.
In soft embraces, nature hums,
A melody of what becomes.

The petals shimmer, bright and fair,
While secrets linger in the air.
With every flutter, dreams arise,
In fleeting glimpses, timeless skies.

The whispering winds through branches flow,
In hidden nooks where wonders grow.
Each echo calls from deep within,
A tale of loss, a tale of kin.

In glimmers soft, the stories weave,
A path unknown, we dare believe.
As shadows stretch and sunlight fades,
The gilded whispers never wade.

With every step in morning light,
The world awakens, pure and bright.
In the wake, the spirit flies,
With gilded whispers, 'neath wide skies.

Celestial Fragments Beneath the Canopy

In twilight hues beneath the trees,
Celestial fragments float with ease.
Stars caught in webs of shadowed dreams,
In nature's cradle, peace redeems.

The canopy whispers secrets old,
In whispers soft, their tales unfold.
Each glimmer sings of worlds afar,
A cosmic dance beneath each star.

Moonlight bathes the forest floor,
In tranquil grace, we yearn for more.
The roots entwined, they hold the past,
In every breath, the die is cast.

Glimmers of fate that softly glow,
In the heart's murmur, wisdom flows.
With every rustle, truths align,
In fragments bright, we seek the divine.

So gaze above, let your heart soar,
In celestial realms, forever explore.
Beneath the canopy, life remains,
In a symphony of joy and pains.

Secrets Hidden in the Woodland's Breath

In the hush of leaves that dance,
Whispers of time hold their stance.
Ancient trees guard secrets near,
Fragments of tales that disappear.

Mossy stones mark hidden trails,
Nature's echo, softest gales.
Roots entwined in a lover's embrace,
In the shadows, dreams interlace.

Sunlight filters through the gray,
Casting warmth to guide the way.
Silent creatures, watchful eyes,
Guard the secrets, old and wise.

With each step, silence calls,
A symphony through timbered halls.
Paths untrodden, stories vast,
In the woodland, shadows cast.

Every breeze sings of the past,
Murmurs of moments that hold fast.
In the heart of green embrace,
Nature's breath, a sacred space.

A Tapestry of Dreams and Dappled Light

Under the canopy, dreams unfold,
Threads of stories, bright yet bold.
Dappled light on the forest floor,
Whispers of hope, now and before.

Golden rays, a painter's brush,
Crafting colors in a hush.
Swaying petals in gentle air,
A tapestry woven with utmost care.

Every leaf tells a tale anew,
Of summer's dance and winter's dew.
Colors mingle, shadows play,
In this gallery, I long to stay.

The air is thick with fragrant blooms,
A chorus rising from nature's rooms.
Softly cradled in twilight's glow,
Dreams of laughter, where breezes blow.

As twilight's veil begins to weave,
A magic that the stars believe.
In this quiet, sacred space,
A tapestry of time and grace.

Foliage of Fantasy Under Celestial Skies

In the embrace of emerald leaves,
Whimsy rests where the heart believes.
Celestial skies, a canvas wide,
Foliage dances as dreams collide.

Moonlit pools, reflections bright,
Hold the wishes of the night.
Stars weave into branches old,
Fables whispered, secrets told.

From ancient bark, stories flow,
Roots unearth what ancients know.
In this haven, magic thrives,
In every breath, our spirit dives.

With each step on this verdant trail,
The world's enchantments never pale.
Fantasies bloom in twilight's rise,
Beneath the splendor of painted skies.

A realm where wishes take to flight,
Under jewels of silver light.
In foliage rich, I find my song,
A fantasy deep, where dreams belong.

Beneath the Boughs of Mythic Shadows

Beneath the boughs where secrets lie,
Legends linger in the sigh.
Mythic shadows stretch and weave,
Stories waiting to believe.

Gnarled roots embrace the ground,
In silence deep, where truths abound.
Every whisper speaks of lore,
Magic echoes forevermore.

Cool, dark havens, the heart aligns,
With stirring dreams and ancient signs.
As twilight wraps its tender arms,
The woodland sprawls with hidden charms.

Flickering lights like fireflies dance,
Lost in the quiet, I find my trance.
In these shadows, mysteries grow,
Beneath the boughs where legends flow.

With every rustle in the night,
Mythic tales take gentle flight.
Under the stars, I lose control,
Beneath the boughs, I find my soul.

Moonlit Shadows on Ancient Boughs

Beneath the moon's gentle glow,
Whispers of night start to flow.
Shadows dance on roots so old,
Secrets of time silently told.

Branches sway in the cool night air,
As memories weave without a care.
Stars twinkle in the vast, dark sea,
Guardian spirits watching, set free.

Mysterious paths where footfalls tread,
Guided by dreams, where hearts are led.
Each sigh of the wind sings a song,
In this twilight where all belong.

The ancient oak cradles the past,
In its arms, shadows are cast.
Echoes of laughter, whispers of fears,
Time folds gently, mingling the years.

So linger a moment, breathe in the night,
Let the shadows weave silk, soft and light.
In moonlit embraces, life finds its way,
Through ancient boughs, forever to stay.

Velvet Colors Amidst the Pines

Soft whispers rustle the pine trees,
As dusk wraps the world with gentle ease.
Velvet colors paint the waning sky,
Where day bids farewell, and dreams fly high.

The forest floor glimmers, rich and deep,
In shadows where the old secrets sleep.
Underneath the aged canopies,
Beauty flourishes, swaying with the breeze.

A canvas of amber, scarlet, and gold,
Nature's treasures silently unfold.
Each hue tells a story, ancient and wise,
Reflecting the heart of the earth's sighs.

In the twilight's embrace, stillness reigns,
Filling the air with sweet refrains.
Every moment a miracle, so divine,
In the velvet glow of the old pine.

With night's gentle hand, the colors blend,
Creating a tapestry that will not end.
In this sacred space, dreams intertwine,
Forever enchanted amidst the pines.

Magic Weaved in Sepia Tones

In sepia tones, the world unfolds,
A nostalgic tale waiting to be told.
Magic lingers in air, soft and sweet,
As time dances lightly on twinkling feet.

The echoes of laughter float through the trees,
As whispers of old secrets hang like a breeze.
Morning dew sparkles with stories of yore,
Remnants of moments that linger and soar.

The fabric of life wears a gentle hue,
Rich like the history of me and of you.
With each passing hour, memories bloom,
Filling our hearts, dispelling the gloom.

In twilight's embrace, we find our way,
Through sepia dreams where shadows play.
Here, within, magic's beauty resides,
In a world where our spirit abides.

So let us explore these colors that gleam,
Chasing the echoes of our shared dream.
Through sepia lenses, we'll always see,
Life's gentle magic, eternally free.

The Chronicles of Sylvan Spirits

In woods where the ancient spirits dwell,
Stories of nature weave a spell.
Chronicles whispered on the breeze,
Holding the wisdom of ancient trees.

Every rustling leaf tells a tale,
Of love and loss, of moments frail.
Sylvan souls drift under moonlight's glow,
Guardians of secrets that only they know.

Through shadows and light, they softly roam,
In harmony with this forest home.
Echoes of laughter, touch of the past,
In each heartbeat, their magic is cast.

Time dances within the canopy's fold,
A vibrant history waiting to be told.
The woodland whispers, treasures await,
In every nook, adventures innate.

So wander through paths both wild and free,
Let the sylvan spirits guide thee.
In their embrace, our hearts shall soar,
As we become part of the lore evermore.

Paintbrushes of the Setting Sun

In the west, the colors blend,
Orange, pink, to the day's end.
Brushes dance with gentle grace,
Strokes of light in vast space.

Clouds like dreams in twilight's glow,
Whispers of the winds that blow.
Nature's masterpiece revealed,
In its beauty, hearts are healed.

The horizon paints anew,
Infinite shades wrapped in dew.
A canvas of warmth and peace,
As day and night find release.

Every hue holds a story tight,
Memories carved in fading light.
With each brush stroke, time will fade,
Yet this moment won't degrade.

As stars twinkle, the sun bids bye,
Its last kiss, a sweet sigh.
In twilight's embrace, the world finds rest,
In the setting sun, we are blessed.

The Forest's Dreamweaver Utters

In shadows deep, the whispers flow,
A secret dance in night's soft glow.
The dreamweaver weaves tales of old,
Of ancient trees and hearts of gold.

Mossy carpets underfoot,
Sprinkling magic, life takes root.
The wind hums low a soothing tune,
Beneath the watchful, silent moon.

Creatures linger, in silence dwell,
Each one carries its own spell.
Rustling leaves share stories bright,
In the heart of the deep, dark night.

A symphony of stars above,
Wraps the forest in gentle love.
Threads of dreams, soft and light,
Guided by the sparkling night.

The dreamweaver stirs, craft ignites,
In every shadow, fresh delights.
As dawn approaches, dreams may fade,
But in the forest, memories stayed.

Twilight's Veil on Nature's Canvas

Twilight drapes its velvet cloak,
On the hills where silence spoke.
Shadows stretch in gentle play,
As the sun bows to end the day.

Brush of dusk on leaves so fair,
Painting whispers in the air.
The brook hums secrets low and clear,
In this moment, nature's near.

Stars peek through, timid and bright,
One by one, they greet the night.
Constellations form their art,
Each a dream, a beating heart.

The sky wears tones of deep indigo,
While crickets start their evening show.
In twilight's grasp, time stands still,
A universe forged by nature's will.

As darkness deepens, mysteries unfold,
Stories of a world untold.
With magic wrapped in a soft embrace,
Twilight's veil, a sacred space.

The Unicorn's Lullaby in Autumn's Grasp

In autumn's chill, a melody sings,
The unicorn prances, ethereal wings.
Golden leaves, like whispers swayed,
Softly falling, a tranquil parade.

Hooves on earth, a gentle beat,
As twilight dances in colors sweet.
The forest listens, holds its breath,
In this moment, life feels fresh.

Stars begin their nightly flight,
Guided by the moon's soft light.
The unicorn's song, pure and bright,
Carries dreams into the night.

With every note, the heart takes wing,
In harmony, the leaves take spring.
A lullaby spun from the past,
In autumn's grip, forever cast.

Through rustling trees, the echoes play,
Of magic found in the light of day.
In the stillness, spirits dance,
Guided gently by romance.

The Spellbound Tales of Amber Twilight

In the hush of dusk, shadows blend,
Golden whispers where dreams ascend.
Stars awaken in the velvet skies,
Painting stories with cosmic sighs.

A breeze carries secrets, old as time,
Melodies echo, sweet as a rhyme.
Glimpses of magic, where hope ignites,
In the heart of the amber twilight.

With each flutter of twilight's grace,
A tapestry woven, a warm embrace.
Softly the world sheds its weary weight,
In the spell of dusk, we contemplate.

Echoes of laughter in fields of gold,
Tales of wonder, forever retold.
Under the glow where the fireflies dance,
Life's gentle stories find their chance.

So linger, dear traveler, in this light,
Let the amber adventures take flight.
For in this moment, dreams intertwine,
In the spellbound tales, your heart will shine.

Mirth Inscribed in Nature's Language

In every leaf, a giggle sways,
The sun beams bright on joyous days.
Petals flutter with laughter pure,
Nature's hymn, a simple cure.

Breezes whisper soft, sweet and low,
Chronicles of life in simple flow.
Streams of joy through valleys run,
In every drop, a story spun.

Clouds frolic as the skies adorned,
Every creature in harmony warned.
In ochre fields where daisies play,
Lies the essence of nature's sway.

Morning calls with a chirping song,
Rays of light where the heart belongs.
Through tangled woods, the joy released,
In nature's language, we find our peace.

So wander where the wildflowers bloom,
Let merriment fill the air with room.
In this vibrant dance of colors bright,
We embrace the mirth of nature's light.

Enigma of the Forest's Colorful Quiet

Beneath the canopy where wonders hide,
Mysteries linger, deep and wide.
Whispers of leaves in muted breath,
A world alive beyond mere death.

Moss carpets the ground, lush and green,
An enigma woven, rarely seen.
Shadows play games in the gentle light,
Painting the forest in hues of night.

Branches murmur in a secret tongue,
Stories of old, forever young.
With every creak, a tale unfolds,
Of ancient magic in whispers bold.

In twilight's embrace, silence flows,
Echoes of beauty in every rose.
Colorful quiet, where spirits roam,
In the heart of the forest, we find our home.

So wander slowly, let wonder guide,
In the tangled woods where secrets bide.
The enigma lies in the stillness found,
In the quiet of nature, peace is crowned.

Songs Grown from Ephemeral Roots

From fleeting moments, melodies rise,
In the soft murmur of summer skies.
Each note a whisper of petals' grace,
Echoing life in a tender space.

Through gardens blooming in vibrant hue,
The songs of the past blend old with new.
Roots intertwine in the soil of dreams,
Flowing like rivers, or so it seems.

The dance of the breezes, the flutter of wings,
In fleeting days, heart's joy it brings.
From ephemeral roots, deep and sincere,
Life's sweet ballads, forever near.

With each dawn's glow, a chorus sings,
Promising hope that tomorrow brings.
In the silence held between each sound,
A symphony of love is found.

So listen closely, let the heart sway,
For songs of the moment will always stay.
In the woven tales of life's gentle shoots,
Lie the cadence of songs, grown from roots.

The Rustic Siren's Song in Fall's Embrace

In amber light the shadows play,
The rustic siren calls the day.
With leaves that dance on gentle air,
Her melody drifts, soft and rare.

Upon the hill where whispers dwell,
The stories of the woods will tell.
In orange hues the branches sway,
As nature's heart begins to sway.

Through golden paths the breezes sing,
Of fleeting time and autumn's wing.
Each note a tale, each tone a sigh,
As seasons turn and moments fly.

Beneath the boughs, the world stands still,
As echoes linger, strong as will.
The siren's song, a haunting grace,
In fall's embrace, our hearts find place.

So let us tread where echoes roam,
In this rich tapestry we call home.
For in her voice, the earth will weave,
A song of hope, for those who believe.

Nature's Jewels in the Crucible of Time

In valleys deep, the treasures hide,
Nature's jewels with grace abide.
Beneath the stars, they sparkle bright,
In darkness whispering soft delight.

The rivers run like silver threads,
Through ancient paths where silence spreads.
Each footprint marks a fleeting tale,
In the crucible, we shall not fail.

The whispers of the winds confide,
In every breeze, our dreams reside.
A symphony of life unfurls,
In the precious dance of worlds.

From mountains high to oceans wide,
Nature's beauty will not hide.
In every leaf and stone so prime,
We find the essence of all time.

So let us marvel, let us see,
The gifts bestowed, so wild and free.
For in this cradle, life will bloom,
Nature's jewels dispel all gloom.

Amber Dreams in Sylvan Skies

In dusk's embrace, the shadows stir,
Amber dreams float, soft and pure.
Through branches wide, the light does stream,
Awakening the heart to dream.

Each whisper sparkles, like the dew,
In sylvan skies of vibrant hue.
The world transforms with falling light,
As day gives way to peaceful night.

In quiet glades, the creatures play,
For dusk unveils a new ballet.
With rustling leaves, the stories blend,
In amber hues, our hearts will mend.

The essence of the forest sings,
In every pulse, the magic clings.
From tree to tree, the spirits glide,
In soft embrace, we all abide.

So let us rest beneath the boughs,
In tranquil peace, we take our vows.
For in this haven, dreams take flight,
Amber dreams await the night.

The Resonance of Whispers in the Grove

In secret glades where shadows dwell,
The resonance of whispers swell.
Among the trees, the stories flow,
In gentle tones, a soft hello.

The wisp of leaves on twilight's breath,
Speaks to us of life and death.
Each rustling sound a tale of yore,
From ancient days to evermore.

The echoes weave through time and space,
Embracing all in warm embrace.
In quiet moments, truths unfold,
The whispers speak of dreams retold.

With every step upon the ground,
The pulse of life, a sacred sound.
In nature's arms, we find our way,
As whispers guide our hearts to stay.

So listen close, let silence reign,
For in this grove, there's much to gain.
The resonance of whispers bright,
Illuminates our path with light.

Harvests of Memory in Autumn's Embrace

Golden leaves whisper soft,
As the sun dips low again.
Fields of corn, now bare,
Hold echoes of our past.

Cider's sweet on the tongue,
Pumpkins smile under the moon.
Scent of woodsmoke lingers,
In the heart of the cool night.

Fires crackle with laughter,
The warmth wraps us like love.
Old stories flow like wine,
Each sip a taste of time.

Harvest moons, bright and full,
Guide us through the deep dark.
Memories dance in shadows,
Painting our dreams anew.

In the chill of the dawn,
Nature breathes a sigh.
We gather golden moments,
In this season of goodbye.

Shimmering Secrets in the Woodland Realm

Beneath the canopy green,
Whispers twine through the leaves.
Sunlight drips like honey,
On paths less traveled by.

Mushrooms bloom near old oaks,
A tapestry of wonder.
Each step hums with magic,
In a dance of shadow and light.

Crickets sing the dusk's lullaby,
While stars peek through the veil.
A brook babbles ancient tales,
Carving the earth with grace.

Squirrels chatter with purpose,
Gathering treasures not seen.
Nature's pulse quickens,
In her twilight embrace.

Secrets weave in the breeze,
As dusk wraps the woodland tight.
The air hums with stories,
Waiting for dawn's soft touch.

The Winding Path of Leaf and Lore

Along the trail we wander,
With leaves of russet and gold.
Each step stirs a whisper,
Of legends left untold.

Footprints blend with memories,
On this path woven with time.
Stories flutter like leaves,
In the wild and fragrant air.

Sunlight dapples the ground,
As shadows stretch and yawn.
Every curve holds a secret,
In the heart of the green wood.

Echoes of laughter linger,
In the sighs of the trees.
Nature cradles our musings,
In the rustle of the pines.

We stroll through fading colors,
As the day begins to wane.
There's magic in this journey,
With each twist and turn we claim.

Twilight's Serenade in Rustling Hues

As twilight drapes the world,
A symphony begins to play.
Crickets hum their evening tune,
While fireflies dance in delight.

The sky blushes in pastels,
Each hue more rich and deep.
Breezes carry a soft sigh,
As day gives way to night.

Trees sway in gentle rhythm,
Their branches whisper low.
The cosmos blinks awake,
In the velvet of the dusk.

Stars emerge like lanterns,
Filling the void with spark.
Moonlight spills on the meadow,
A quilt of silver and dreams.

In this sanctuary of dusk,
We breathe in the magic.
Each moment lingers softly,
In twilight's tender embrace.

Glimmers Beneath the Celestial Boughs

Soft whispers dance through flowing leaves,
Stars peek down, where the night deceives.
Moonlit paths guide our gentle way,
In dreams we wander, where shadows play.

Flickering lights in the hush of dusk,
Nature's breath, sweet as musk.
Each twinkle shows a tale untold,
Glimmers of life in the night unfold.

Under the boughs, where secrets lie,
We find our peace beneath the sky.
Moments linger in twilight's hue,
In silence, we savor all that's true.

The rustle of leaves sings a song,
In this enchanted grove, we belong.
Finding the magic in each new glance,
Together here, we sway and dance.

As dawn awakens the slumbering night,
The glimmers fade, replaced by light.
Yet memories stay, like whispers clear,
Beneath celestial boughs, forever near.

Echoes of the Forest's Cloak

In the forest deep, where silence thrives,
Echoes pulse, where the spirit dives.
A cloak of green drapes every sound,
Mysteries linger all around.

Branches weave tales of days gone by,
Each rustling leaf a soft goodbye.
Time itself seems to pause and sigh,
In hues of green, the memories lie.

Birdsong flutters like sweet refrains,
Each call a thread that gently remains.
While shadows stretch and daylight wanes,
An orchestra dwells where nature reigns.

Mossy carpets cradle our tread,
Stories whisper where the wild things fed.
In this sacred space, we lose our way,
As echoes guide us through the day.

The forest breathes, a timeless sea,
Wrapped in peace, we're wild and free.
In every echo, we find our place,
In the forest's cloak, a warm embrace.

Gilded Moments in a Sylvan Realm

In a sylvan realm where light does play,
Gilded moments slip away.
Sunbeams filter through the trees,
Dancing softly in the breeze.

Golden hues paint every leaf,
Nature's brush creates belief.
Time's embrace in glimmers bright,
In this hush, the world feels right.

Whispers drift on the fragrant air,
Memories linger everywhere.
Each heartbeat syncs with nature's song,
In this space, we feel we belong.

Petals fall like soft-spun gold,
Stories shared, forever told.
Together, we weave our dreams anew,
In gilded moments, bright and true.

As twilight crowns the day's embrace,
We cherish warmth in this sacred place.
In the golden glow, we find our peace,
In sylvan realms, our hearts release.

Tales in Tints of Gold and Mysticism

Tales unfold in shadowed glens,
Where golden light meets whispers' spins.
Mysticism hangs in the air,
Each story cradled with utmost care.

In the twilight's gentle hold,
Nature shares its secrets bold.
Every petal, every stone,
Carries magic, softly grown.

The sun dips low, igniting dreams,
Among the branches, warm light beams.
Crickets chirp their evening song,
In this twilight, we belong.

Stars awaken with a glimmering gaze,
Illuminating hidden ways.
In hues of gold, we find our path,
Unraveling nature's swirling wrath.

So here we sit, in peace entwined,
Tales of wonder, softly outlined.
In the realm of gold and misty lore,
We discover worlds to explore.

Where Mystical Creatures Wander

In twilight's glow, shadows dance,
Elusive forms in a secret trance.
Whispers weave through the ancient trees,
Where dreams take flight on a gentle breeze.

Fae and sprites in ethereal light,
Glistening wings in the soft moonlight.
Echoes of laughter, a sweet embrace,
Lost in a world, a forgotten place.

They gather where the wildflowers bloom,
Under the stars, they vanish like gloom.
With every step, magic ignites,
Mystical creatures chase the night flights.

In the hush, their stories unfurl,
Legends whispered, dreams to unfurl.
Through woods aglow with a silvery sheen,
A realm unseen, yet softly serene.

As dawn approaches, the shadows retract,
Nature's whispers in silence intact.
Yet in our hearts, their essence stays,
Where magical legacies dance and play.

A Tapestry of Twilight and Dreams

Threads of dusk knit the night sky,
Painting the clouds with colors shy.
Stars like jewels, twinkling bright,
A canvas alive in soft twilight.

Dreams weave gently in the cool air,
Whispers of hopes, both subtle and rare.
Silver moonlight spills on the ground,
A lullaby's echo, a soft, sweet sound.

In shadows deep, visions take flight,
Ethereal echoes in the heart of night.
As time drifts softly, lost in a haze,
We dance in the twilight's mesmerizing maze.

Every moment, a delicate thread,
Binding our dreams in the world we tread.
A tapestry woven with care and grace,
In the twilight's embrace, we find our place.

As dawn creeps in, and colors fade,
Memories linger in the moments made.
A tapestry stitched with love, it seems,
Forever alive in our waking dreams.

The Secrets Beneath the Canopy

Whispers hidden in the emerald leaves,
Nature's secrets, the heart believes.
Beneath the canopy's protective veil,
Stories unfold in the softest trail.

Moss carpets the ground, lush and green,
Every step echoes where they've been.
Creatures slumber in daylight's hold,
Guarding the tales of the brave and bold.

The gentle rustle speaks of old lore,
Of ancients who gathered, who came before.
Roots intertwined in a dance so grand,
Binding together the earth and land.

Through dappled light, mysteries hide,
In the cool shade, where shadows bide.
With each heartbeat, the forest sighs,
Revealing the magic that never dies.

As twilight descends, the secrets awake,
In the silence, the earth starts to break.
The whispers grow louder, the stories unfold,
Beneath the canopy, a treasure untold.

Celestial Veil of Rustic Hues

A canvas woven with rustic tones,
Where earth meets sky, and time condones.
Golden fields under the setting sun,
Embraced by twilight, the day is done.

Clouds drift softly, a celestial show,
Washing the land in a gentle glow.
Cascading colors, they blend and fuse,
Creating a veil of tranquil hues.

Whispers of wind through the autumn trees,
Rustling leaves in a symphonic breeze.
Nature's orchestra plays a sweet tune,
Beneath the watchful, glowing moon.

Mysteries linger in the still air,
Crafting a world beautiful and rare.
With every heartbeat, the universe sighs,
A celestial dance beneath endless skies.

As night unfolds with a tender grace,
Stars emerge, each one a face.
In the rustic hues, our dreams align,
Under the celestial veil, hearts entwine.

When Fantasy Meets the Forest Floor

In the woods where whispers sigh,
Mossy beds and shadows lie.
Fairy lights twinkle bright,
Guiding dreams into the night.

Ancient trees in silence stand,
Guardians of this mystic land.
Footsteps soft on leafy trails,
Woven tales of wind and gales.

Beneath the boughs, magic swirls,
Capturing hearts and dreams of girls.
A gentle breeze, a rustling sound,
Nature's secrets all around.

Elven laughter fills the air,
As moonlight dances everywhere.
In the glen where shadows roam,
Every heart can find a home.

So wander forth where fantasies weave,
In the forest, dare to believe.
For every path and whispered lore,
Awaits the magic on the floor.

Hues of Enchantment in the Golden Hour

As sunlight spills in amber glow,
The world is bathed in hues below.
Crimson leaves in gentle sway,
Heralding the close of day.

Shadows stretch and softly blend,
Whispering tales that twilight send.
Gold and rust, a painter's dream,
Nature dons her jeweled gleam.

In the fields where daisies dance,
Magic thrives in every glance.
The sky ignites with fiery flair,
An artist's brush strokes everywhere.

The breeze carries a sweet perfume,
As flowers bask in twilight's bloom.
Chasing clouds, the colors play,
Serenading the end of day.

In this moment, hearts align,
Finding peace in nature's design.
As night descends with quiet grace,
We hold this dusk, a sacred space.

Songs of the Sylvan Serpent

In twilight's hush, a serpent sings,
Between the pines and whispered things.
With scales of gold and emerald sheen,
It glides through realms both felt and seen.

A melody of leaves in flight,
By silver moon and starlit night.
It twists and turns, a dance of grace,
In nature's heart, it finds its place.

Echoes of stories intertwined,
In the forest's depths, wisdom entwined.
With every note, a spell is cast,
Binding futures with echoes past.

Secrets held in every scale,
The serpent whispers soft, yet pale.
Through thickets lush and shadows deep,
It sings the dreams we long to keep.

So listen close to what it shares,
In leafy glades where magic flares.
For every song that finds its way,
Is a promise of a new day.

Autumn's Palette on Fairy Wings

In gardens rich with crimson hues,
Where fairies dance in morning dew.
With every flutter, colors blend,
A tapestry the seasons send.

Golden glimmers start to fade,
As rustling leaves in pathways laid.
With tender grace, the fairies play,
Painting dreams before decay.

Sweet whispers carried by the breeze,
Amongst the branches of aging trees.
They craft a canvas, bold and bright,
In nature's gallery of light.

Each brushstroke frayed with time's embrace,
A story woven in greens and lace.
As petals drift on autumn's sigh,
The fairies' laughter lifts to the sky.

So celebrate the fleeting show,
As colors dance and softly glow.
With wings of magic, spirits sing,
Of autumn's art, the joy they bring.

Fables Woven in Rich Rust

In fields where stories breathe and grow,
The whispers of the old winds blow.
With each grain, a tale unfolds,
In twilight hues, the past retolds.

Beneath the trees that arch and sway,
Their branches dance in bright array.
The laughter of the leaves resounds,
Echoing where magic abounds.

As sunset spills its golden thread,
The night draws near, and dreams are fed.
In fragile webs, the fables bind,
While shadows wrap the heart and mind.

From rusted hues, the stories weave,
A tapestry no eyes perceive.
In whispers soft, the secrets flow,
And linger in the afterglow.

Harvest Moonlight on Whistling Leaves

The harvest moon rides high and bright,
Casting a charm with silver light.
Beneath its gaze, the world does sing,
As leaves begin their gentle fling.

The branches sway with softest grace,
Embracing night's warm, sweet embrace.
A symphony of rustling sound,
In nature's breath, our hearts are found.

The glowing orb lights up the path,
Where shadows dance, and echoes laugh.
In this sacred, tranquil space,
Harvest dreams find their rightful place.

The leaves do whistle in the breeze,
A playful tune that brings us ease.
In moonlit fields, our spirits soar,
Connected deep, forevermore.

Enchantment Beneath the Arbor's Whisper

Beneath the trees, enchantments weave,
In whispered tales that hearts believe.
The dappled light, a soft caress,
In nature's arms, our souls find rest.

Each rustling leaf, a secret shared,
A promise spoken, gently dared.
In twilight's glow, the magic hums,
As evening breathes, and stillness comes.

The roots entwined in earth's embrace,
In time's soft hands, we find our place.
With every sigh, the world awakes,
In harmony, the spirit shakes.

As stars begin to dot the sky,
Under this bough, we long to lie.
In nature's cradle, we are free,
Enchanted by serenity.

The Ethereal Dance of Nature's Palette

The canvas broad, the colors blend,
Nature's brush strokes never end.
In morning's light, soft hues ignite,
As day unveils its vibrant sight.

From blooms that sway in summer's grace,
To autumn's weave, a bold embrace.
The seasons paint in rich delight,
An ethereal dance, pure and bright.

With every shade, a story told,
In splashes warm and splatters bold.
A kaleidoscope before our eyes,
Where beauty lives, and wonder lies.

As winter cloaks in silver frost,
An artist's heart, no dream is lost.
Through nature's palette wide and true,
The dance continues, always new.

Fabled Glimmers in the Thicket

In shadows deep, where secrets dwell,
Fabled glimmers weave their spell.
Beneath the leaves, a story stirs,
Whispers of magic in gentle blurs.

Silent creatures dance with grace,
As twilight drapes its silken lace.
Every rustle, every sigh,
Hints at wonders passing by.

Golden light just brushes through,
Painting dreams in vibrant hue.
Lost in tales of time gone by,
Here, the heart learns how to fly.

Each step a secret, each turn a chance,
Nature's music, an ancient dance.
With every breath, the woods awake,
In fabled glimmers, hearts will break.

So wander deep, let spirits roam,
In thickets lush, you'll find a home.
Where magic lives and shadows play,
Fabled glimmers guide the way.

Echoes of the Mythical Grove

In the grove where moments sleep,
Echoes swirl in silence deep.
Myths and legends interlace,
In every corner, every space.

Tall trees whisper tales of old,
Of heroes brave and hearts of gold.
Amongst the roots, the stories throng,
A timeless echo, a haunting song.

The gentle breeze, a messenger,
Of dreams departed, and love's stir.
Leaves will tell of paths once walked,
In shadows where the ancients talked.

Moonlight bathes the forest floor,
Unlocks the dreams, opens the door.
Here in the grove, the spirits blend,
In echoes, beginnings meet their end.

So linger where the past unspools,
In mythical glades, we find the rules.
To listen keen, the hearts will show,
The echoes of a grove aglow.

Ferns and Fables in a Woodland Requiem

Ferns unfurl in emerald grace,
Whispering soft, they find their place.
Among the shadows, stories sleep,
In woodland wonders, secrets keep.

A requiem of time's embrace,
Fables linger in this space.
Each rustling leaf, a ghostly tune,
Sings of dusk and the rising moon.

Branches bow with tales of bliss,
Nature's beauty in every hiss.
In twilight's glow, all comes alive,
Where ferns and fables come to thrive.

The air is thick with memories bright,
A tapestry woven with day and night.
Here nestled deep, the heart takes flight,
In the woodland's breath, we find our light.

So gather close, let silence reign,
In ferns and fables, love's sweet pain.
Where every story finds its end,
In woodland requiem, we transcend.

The Whisper of Forgotten Paths

A whisper calls through tangled vines,
Forgotten paths in ancient signs.
Where footfalls fade and silence sighs,
The past unfolds beneath blue skies.

Each turn reveals a tale untold,
In every shadow, a heart of gold.
Time meanders like a gentle stream,
In whispers lost, we chase a dream.

The wildflowers bloom, the echoes ring,
As nature breathes, our spirits sing.
Amongst the duff, the memories lie,
In whispered paths where dreams can fly.

So tread with care through woods unseen,
Discover realms where few have been.
The tender embrace of what has passed,
Will guide you home, forever cast.

Embrace the chance, let go the fears,
In whispered light, dry all your tears.
For on forgotten paths we tread,
The whispers hold the love we've shed.

www.ingramcontent.com/pod-product-compliance
Ingram Content Group UK Ltd.
Pitfield, Milton Keynes, MK11 3LW, UK
UKHW021646160125
4146UKWH00033B/619

9 781805 599845